THIS BOOK BELONGS TO

_____

FOR THE KIDS WHO SECRETLY
WANT A FRIEND

ISBN: 9798894581880

IT WAS CHRISTMAS EVE, AND EMMA, A SHY GIRL WITH ROSY CHEEKS
AND BIG BLUE EYES, STOOD ALONE IN HER SNOWY BACKYARD.
SHE SIGHED, WATCHING HER NEIGHBORS LAUGH AND PLAY.

FEELING LONELY, EMMA BEGAN TO ROLL A SNOWBALL.
"IF ONLY I HAD A FRIEND," SHE WHISPERED, HER BREATH
TURNING TO FROST IN THE CHILLY AIR.

SHE WORKED TIRELESSLY, SHAPING THE SNOW INTO A SNOWMAN.
SHE GAVE HIM A CARROT NOSE, A CROOKED SCARF, AND SHINY PEBBLE EYES.

THE MOON ROSE HIGH, CASTING A SILVERY GLOW.
EMMA STEPPED BACK TO ADMIRE HER SNOWMAN.
"MERRY CHRISTMAS, MR. FROST," SHE SAID SOFTLY.

SUDDENLY, A GUST OF WIND SWIRLED AROUND THE SNOWMAN,
AND HIS PEBBLE EYES TWINKLED.
"DID YOU JUST CALL ME MR. FROST?" A CHEERFUL VOICE ASKED.

EMMA GASPED AS THE SNOWMAN CAME TO LIFE,
STRETCHING HIS STICK ARMS. "YOU'RE ALIVE?" SHE STAMMERED.

"OF COURSE!" HE CHUCKLED.
"CHRISTMAS EVE MAGIC IS MY FAVORITE THING.
WHAT'S YOUR NAME?"

"I'M EMMA," SHE SAID, HER LONELINESS MELTING
LIKE SNOW IN THE SUN. "CAN WE... BE FRIENDS?"

"FRIENDS? ABSOLUTELY!" MR. FROST SAID, TIPPING AN IMAGINARY HAT.
"WHAT SHOULD WE DO FIRST?"

"LET'S EXPLORE!" EMMA SUGGESTED. SHE LED MR. FROST THROUGH HER SNOWY YARD, POINTING OUT HER FAVORITE SPOTS.

THEY SLID ACROSS THE FROZEN POND, LAUGHING AS
MR. FROST TWIRLED LIKE A DANCER, HIS SCARF FLAPPING BEHIND HIM.

"I'VE NEVER ICE-SKATED BEFORE!" MR. FROST EXCLAIMED,
WOBBLING ON INVISIBLE SKATES.

NEXT, THEY BUILT ANOTHER SNOWMAN, A "FRIEND" FOR MR. FROST.
"THE MORE, THE MERRIER!" HE SAID.

THEY LAY ON THE GROUND, MAKING SNOW ANGELS.
MR. FROST'S SNOW ANGEL LOOKED MORE LIKE A LUMPY STAR.
"IT'S PERFECT!" EMMA LAUGHED.

AS THE NIGHT GREW COLDER, MR. FROST SAID, "LET'S SEE THE TOWN!"
EMMA HESITATED BUT NODDED, CURIOSITY SPARKLING IN HER EYES.

THEY WANDERED THROUGH THE QUIET, SNOWY STREETS.
CHRISTMAS LIGHTS TWINKLED IN EVERY WINDOW,
FILLING EMMA'S HEART WITH WARMTH.

MR. FROST STOPPED IN FRONT OF A BRIGHTLY DECORATED HOUSE.
"WHAT'S THAT WONDERFUL SMELL?" HE ASKED.

"IT'S GINGERBREAD!" EMMA SAID. "COME ON, LET'S PEEK INSIDE."

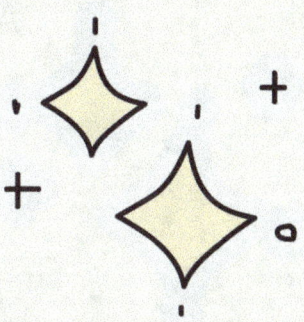

THROUGH THE WINDOW, THEY SAW A FAMILY LAUGHING
AROUND A TABLE COVERED IN COOKIES AND MILK.

EMMA'S SMILE FALTERED. "I WISH I HAD A FAMILY LIKE THAT,"
SHE WHISPERED.

"YOU DO," MR. FROST SAID GENTLY. "YOUR FAMILY IS JUST WAITING FOR YOU TO SHARE YOUR CHRISTMAS SPIRIT WITH THEM."

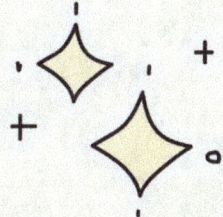

EMMA LOOKED THOUGHTFUL. "MAYBE YOU'RE RIGHT," SHE SAID SOFTLY.

THEY CONTINUED THEIR JOURNEY, PASSING A PARK WHERE
A LONE SLED SAT ATOP A HILL.

"LET'S RIDE!" MR. FROST SAID. EMMA CLIMBED IN, AND WITH A PUSH, THEY ZOOMED DOWN THE HILL, SQUEALING WITH JOY.

AT THE BOTTOM, THEY COLLAPSED INTO GIGGLES, SNOWFLAKES
CLINGING TO EMMA'S HAIR AND MR. FROST'S SCARF.

AS MIDNIGHT APPROACHED, THE STARS SPARKLED BRIGHTER,
AND A SOFT BELL RANG IN THE DISTANCE.

"IT'S ALMOST CHRISTMAS DAY!" MR. FROST SAID, HIS VOICE TINGED WITH SADNESS. "I DON'T HAVE MUCH TIME LEFT."

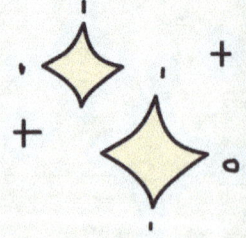

EMMA'S HEART SANK. "YOU'RE LEAVING?"

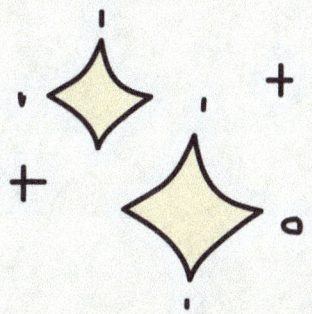

"I HAVE TO," MR. FROST SAID. "BUT I'LL ALWAYS BE WITH YOU.
ANYTIME YOU NEED ME, JUST BUILD A SNOWMAN."

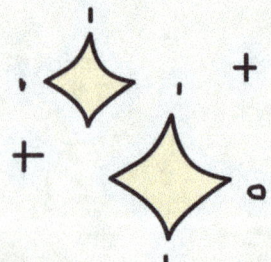

EMMA HUGGED HIM TIGHTLY, FEELING THE CHILL OF HIS SNOWY FRAME. "I'LL NEVER FORGET YOU," SHE SAID.

AS THE FIRST RAYS OF CHRISTMAS MORNING DAWNED,
MR. FROST'S EYES TWINKLED ONE LAST TIME.
"MERRY CHRISTMAS, EMMA," HE SAID BEFORE FADING INTO THE SNOW.

EMMA SAT QUIETLY, WATCHING THE SUNRISE. THE YARD FELT EMPTY BUT WARM, AS IF MR. FROST'S SPIRIT LINGERED.

EMMA RAN INSIDE, HER CHEEKS GLOWING.
SHE HUGGED HER PARENTS TIGHTLY, SURPRISING THEM.

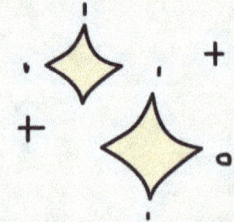

"LET'S MAKE THIS THE BEST CHRISTMAS EVER!"
EMMA SAID, HER HEART FULL OF JOY.

THE FAMILY SPENT THE DAY LAUGHING, BAKING COOKIES, AND EXCHANGING GIFTS.

EMMA STEPPED OUTSIDE THAT EVENING AND GAZED AT THE SNOWY YARD.
"THANK YOU, MR. FROST," SHE WHISPERED.

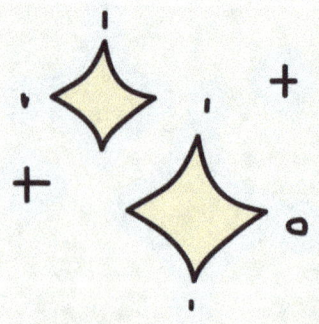

THE WIND SWIRLED GENTLY, CARRYING A FAINT LAUGH, AND EMMA SMILED.

THE MOON ROSE HIGH AGAIN, CASTING A SILVERY GLOW.
IN THE CORNER OF THE YARD, EMMA BEGAN BUILDING ANOTHER SNOWMAN.

SHE PLACED A CARROT FOR THE NOSE AND POLISHED PEBBLES FOR THE EYES. "SEE YOU NEXT CHRISTMAS, MR. FROST," SHE SAID SOFTLY.

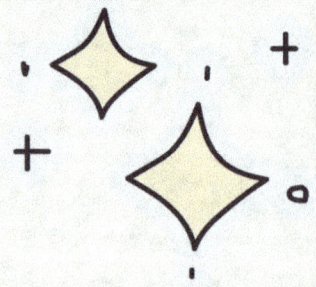

THE SNOWMAN STOOD TALL UNDER THE STARRY SKY, AND IN THE DISTANCE, A BELL CHIMED, WELCOMING THE MAGIC OF THE SEASON.

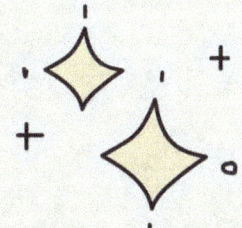

MAKE SURE TO TAKE A LOOK AT MY OTHER CHRISTMAS BOOKS FOR KIDS